Tell me about...

Rugby

Published in 2009 by Evans Publishing Ltd,
2A Portman Mansions,
Chiltern St, London WIU 6NR

Editor: Nicola Edwards
Designer: D.R. Ink
All photos by Wishlist except for p6 Tim Smith/Getty Images; p7(t) Tom Shaw/Getty Images, p7(b) Getty Images for Yazoo; p8 Clive Rose/Getty Images; p12 Shaun Botterill/Getty Images; p13 Stu Forster/Getty Images; p14 Warren Little/Getty Images; p17 David Rogers/Getty Images; p19 David Rogers/Getty Images; p21 Tim Smith/Getty Images; p23 PATRICK KOVARIK/AFP/Getty Images; p24 Photo by Matt King/Getty Images; p26 JACQUES DEMARTHON/AFP/Getty Images; p27Mark Nolan/Getty Images

British Library Cataloguing in Publication Data

Gifford, Clive
  Rugby. - (Tell me about sport)
  1. Rugby football -- Juvenile literature.
  I. Title II. Series
  796. 3'33 - dc22

ISBN-13: 9780237538972

Printed in China.

The author and publisher would like to thank Isiah Rudkin, Aaron Taylor, Fergus Wood, Jake Anderson George Grieve, Reece Lines, Simon Grieve - coach and Banbury RFC for their help in making this book.

Contents

Rugby

▲
Attack and defence meet here, with the player carrying the ball tackled by an opponent. Rugby does contain lots of impacts and contacts, but players must always play fairly so they don't harm an opponent.

Power, pace, breathtaking skills and crunching collisions are all part of the great game of rugby. There are several codes of rugby including rugby league which features 13 players in a team. This book is all about the wonderful world of rugby union – a team sport for 15 players a side.

Rugby union is played in over 100 countries around the world and its World Cup, held every four years, is a massive competition. During the 2007 Rugby World Cup which was held in France, Scotland and Wales, 1.6 million people watched live games and hundreds of millions more tuned in on television.

▲ Players wear gumshields to protect their teeth. Some wear a padded hat called a scrumcap to protect their head and ears as well.

▼ Tag rugby is an exciting type of mini rugby. The player with the ball is tackled if one of the tags (pieces of cloth) from her belt is removed. She must stop moving and pass the ball in three seconds and then pick up her tag.

A full game of rugby lasts for two halves of 40 minutes each. The sport has many rules yet, at its heart, it's a simple game. Players kick, run with or pass an oval-shaped ball in order to move up the pitch to score tries. Players in the team without the ball try to stop the other team's progress and win the ball back so that they can attack.

You can get into rugby at almost any age. Many rugby clubs run special days or after-school sessions for boys and, sometimes, girls. Many players start out by playing forms of mini rugby on a smaller pitch and with simpler rules. As well as being great fun to play, mini rugby allows you to develop important passing, catching and running skills.

Scoring a try

Scoring tries is what rugby is all about. The referee awards a try when an attacking player grounds the ball in the other team's in-goal area. The player has to press the ball down on the ground for it to count as a try. The try isn't given if the player's foot, or any other part of the body, is touching the ground outside the line of the pitch.

▼ The player in the striped shirt has dived for the line to score a try. The goal line counts as part of the in-goal area.

A try is worth five points. The try-scoring team then has a chance to score an extra two points with a conversion kick. The kick is taken in line with where the try was scored. This is why try-scorers try to run behind the goal posts before they ground the ball. They aim to give their team's kicker an easier kick.

A penalty is awarded by a referee when a team breaks the rules. The team given a penalty may choose to kick for goal. The kick is taken just like a conversion kick but is worth three, not two, points.

▲ A drop goal is worth three points. It is scored in regular play when a player drop-kicks the ball between the goal posts. In Rugby Sevens (see page 27), this is the style of kick used to score conversions as well.

▼ Conversion and penalty kicks are taken with the ball sitting up on a plastic tee. The kicker takes a short run up and strikes firmly through the ball with a long follow-through. He scores if the ball sails between the uprights and over the bar.

The pitch and team

A rugby pitch is a large rectangle of grass split into two halves by a halfway line. Either side of the halfway line is a 10m line. The ball has to travel at least 10 metres forward from a kick-off, so the 10m line provides a useful guide for referees.

The main part of the pitch is 100m long. At each end is an in-goal area, marked at the front by the try line. The in-goal area is between 10m and 22m deep and is where players can score tries.

The 22m line is 22 metres from the front of each in-goal area. Players who catch the ball in their own 22 can kick the ball straight out over a sideline. Play re-starts at the point on the sideline where the ball left the pitch.

▼ This is a full-sized rugby pitch with one team lining up on it.

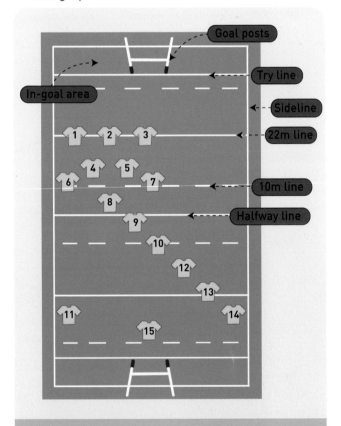

Goal posts
Try line
In-goal area
Sideline
22m line
10m line
Halfway line

1. Loosehead Prop
2. Hooker
3. Tighthead Prop
4. Second Row
5. Second Row
6. Blindside Flanker
7. Openside Flanker
8. Number 8
9. Scrum Half
10. Fly Half
11. Left Winger
12. Inside Centre
13. Outside Centre
14. Right Winger
15. Fullback

A rugby team is split into eight forwards and seven backs. The forwards aim to gain the ball and take part in scrums and lineouts (see p22). The scrum half is the back with the job of taking the ball from the forwards and passing to the rest of the backs. The fly half is the team's key decision-maker who chooses most often whether to run with the ball, kick it or pass it.

▲
A player shouts "Mark!" whilst making a high catch. As he is inside his own 22, the other team has to stop and retreat, giving the player time and space to kick the ball.

During a match, a rugby team can make replacements in a similar way to how substitutes are made in a game of football.

▼ Strong defensive play has pushed the player with the ball over the sideline. This means that the game will restart with a lineout with the throw-in made by the other team.

Rugby superstars

Top rugby players are professional sports stars. They are paid to play and the very best, such as Ireland's Brian O'Driscoll, New Zealand's Dan Carter, Shane Williams of Wales and South Africa's Bryan Habana, become famous.

Behind the glamour, players need to work very hard if they want to be the best. Rugby demands incredible strength, speed and fitness. Players have to train hard.

▼ Irish full back, Geordan Murphy (on the left) and Welsh winger, Shane Williams (on the right) use a tackle pad in training. Williams is Wales' leading try scorer and in 2008 was voted the International Rugby Board's Player of the Year.

▲ Stirling Mortlock of Australia is helped off the field with an injury during a 2008 match against Wales.

Injuries are common and can be frustrating as players sit out games and work with a physiotherapist and other medical staff to recover.

The best players play for their country. England, France, Ireland, Italy, Scotland and Wales play in the Six Nations tournament every year. South Africa, Australia and New Zealand play in a similar competition called the Tri-Nations. In addition, there are tours to other countries and, once every four years, the prospect of playing in the biggest rugby competition of all, the Rugby World Cup.

Top players

George Gregan played for Australia a record 139 times, more than any other player.

England's Jason Leonard holds the record for the forward who has played the most times in internationals, with 114 games for England.

After winning the 2003 Rugby World Cup with England, Jonny Wilkinson suffered 11 separate injuries over the next three years. He had an amazing 1,167 days of treatment.

Passing and catching

Passing and catching are among the most vital skills you will learn in rugby. They are so important, that top players continue to practise handling the ball every day. Rugby coaches show players how to work on and improve these skills.

All passes in rugby must be sideways across the pitch or backwards. If you make a forward pass, the referee will signal it and usually awards a scrum (see pages 22-23). The other team will put the ball into the scrum. The same will happen if you fumble the ball when trying to catch it and knock it forward.

▼ There are other types of pass. Here, the scrum half, Junior Polu of Samoa, makes a diving pass from the base of a scrum.

▲ This is the basic, lateral pass – the most common pass in rugby. The player swings his arms across his body and releases the ball with a snap of his wrists.

When passing, players concentrate on having a good grip on the ball. They must release it so that it travels at the perfect height and speed for their team-mate to catch. Players receiving the ball stretch out their fingers and watch the ball until it is in their hands. Receivers bring the ball into their body to hold it securely.

Good passing can open up a defence. Top players try all sorts of passing moves including long passes which miss out several of their team-mates and move the ball rapidly to another part of the pitch. These can be risky as a long pass may be intercepted by an opponent who may then run with the ball and score a try.

Pass it on

During the 2006 Wales v Australia match the teams completed 189 passes. The game ended in a thrilling 29-29 draw.

At the 2002 London Marathon, a team of 10 rugby players ran the entire 42.2km race passing a ball between them without dropping it!

Attacking

Attacking needs both great individual skills and a lot of good teamwork. Players rarely score a try all by themselves. The ball is usually passed between players as they look for a gap in the other team's defence.

Players with the ball must run hard but keep their head up to spot where team-mates are and where danger lies. A player can use various skills to get past a defender including the hand-off and sidesteps where the player pushes off one foot and lurches sideways.

▼ This player makes a dummy pass. He looks as if he will pass to his team-mate and the defender shifts his balance towards the receiver. At the last moment, the player draws the ball quickly back in to his body and swerves around the defender.

▲ This scissors pass changes the direction of the ball suddenly. The two players run different lines and as they cross, a short pass is made.

▲
England forward Lee Mears has spotted a gap in the defence and is sprinting through. He can use the open palm of his hand to push away an opponent. This is called a hand-off.

Attackers without the ball support their team-mate by running into positions to receive a pass. If a team-mate is tackled, attackers aim to reach the scene before an opposing player to retrieve the ball.

Young players are encouraged to keep hold of the ball. Adult players sometimes use kicks in attack. For instance, they might chip the ball over a row of defenders for a team-mate to run onto.

Tackling

Tackling the player with the ball is a major part of a full game of rugby. It involves impact but when taught and practised well, will not hurt or cause injury. A coach will take you through tackling skills and explain all the key safety points.

Most tackles are made between the knees and stomach of an opponent. A good tackle stops an opponent in his or her tracks and will usually bring you both to the ground. You must let go of the player once you've made the tackle and try to roll away. If you do not, the referee will award the other team a penalty.

▼ This player makes a good side tackle. His shoulder connects with the other player's waist and his arms wrap round the player. He makes sure he gets his head behind the tackled player. Both players fall to the ground.

▲ Tackle training can be great fun. Here, players practise a front-on tackle using padded tackle bags. The players get their heads to one side of the bag and shrug their shoulder as they make impact.

▼ The defender makes a tap tackle used when a regular tackle cannot be made. The tackler uses his hand to make a firm tap of his opponent's ankle causing him to trip and fall.

There are other parts to defence apart from tackling. It's important to be aware of where the runners in the other team are. This means keeping in position so that you can make a tackle should an opponent near to you get the ball. Defenders also look out for chances to intercept a pass or charge down (or block) the other team's kicks.

Keeping the ball

Keeping the ball is crucial to attacking and scoring points. Players in a team try their hardest to keep possession of the ball when one of their team is tackled.

When you are tackled you must release the ball. Sometimes, it is possible to twist and turn and make a short pass, called an offload, to a team-mate. Most often, you will head to the floor along with the tackler. You must then let go of the ball or the referee will award a penalty against your team.

▼ This tackled player has turned to face his own team and places the ball back before letting go. He gives his team-mates the best possible chance to keep possession.

▼ This player has been stopped by a tackler but his arms are free enough for him to make an offload pass.

The French women's team have driven hard in a ruck to win the ball from Ireland at the 2006 Women's World Cup. The French scrum half, Julie Pujol, is able to pick up the ball and fire off a pass.

Both teams may now contest the ball but only under strict rules. A ruck forms when players from both sides come into contact over the ball. Players from one team try to drive the other team's players back. If successful, one of their team-mates will run in from behind to collect the ball.

A maul is a little like a ruck but occurs when the tackled player stays on his feet. Players from both teams join round the player with the ball and try to drive the other team back.

Scrums and lineouts

Scrums and lineouts are two major ways of restarting a game of rugby. They are quite complicated with lots of rules, but they can be fascinating contests of strength, timing and skill.

▲ The team's hooker is in charge of throwing the ball in at the lineout. He holds the ball with its pointed end forward and tries to throw it at the right height and distance.

Lineouts occur when the ball has gone out of play over the sidelines. The referee awards the throw-in to the team who didn't touch the ball last. A row of players from each team lines up with a metre gap between the rows. The ball has to be thrown straight down this gap. The jumpers, usually the tallest players in the team, compete to reach the ball.

This scrum half is feeding the ball into a scrum. If he does not put the ball in straight, the scrum put-in goes to the other team. A scrum has three players per side at under-10 level and eight at under-13s and above.

Scrums are awarded for many things including when the ball is knocked on or passed forward, or when players carry the ball over their own try line. The eight forwards on a team bind together and then engage with the other team's forwards to form a tunnel down the middle.

The ball is put in to the tunnel by the scrum half and struck back by the foot of the hooker (see page 10). It travels back to the feet of the number 8 – the player at the back of the scrum. The number 8 controls the ball and can pick it up to run with it or pass it. Alternatively the number 8 allows the scrum half to collect the ball.

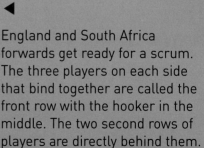

England and South Africa forwards get ready for a scrum. The three players on each side that bind together are called the front row with the hooker in the middle. The two second rows of players are directly behind them.

Rugby rules...OK!

Rugby's rules are really involved but a good teacher or coach will help young players understand them. Knowing how the game works is crucial to becoming a good rugby player.

A rugby game is run by a referee and two assistants called touch judges. The touch judges run the sidelines during the match except when a kick at goal is being made. Then, they stand behind the goal to see if the ball went through or not.

▼ The referee is signalling to the players that a high tackle has been made.

24

Referees try to keep a game going but have to blow their whistle if a team breaks the game's rules. This may result in a scrum or lineout or in a penalty.

Players respect the referee as he or she keeps the game safe for the players. A player who argues with a referee, or plays unfairly or dangerously, is likely to be shown a yellow card. This means the player has to leave the pitch for the sin bin for ten minutes. A player who is shown a red card is sent off the pitch for the rest of the game.

▲ The player with the ball has run directly into his team-mate. This is called accidental obstruction. The other team will get the put-in at a scrum.

▼ A referee will signal a knock-on as this player drops the ball and nudges it forward.

▼ As he runs to score a try, the player with the ball is tripped deliberately by an opponent's foot. The defender is in trouble and will be sent to the sin bin.

The world of rugby

▲ England winger Paul Sackey is tackled by South Africa's Bryan Habana in the 2007 Rugby World Cup Final. South Africa won 15-9 whilst Habana scored an amazing eight tries throughout the tournament.

Rugby is played at all levels from schools and local clubs right up to international rugby where players represent their country. Countries as far apart as Argentina, Georgia, Japan, and the United States all have national teams.

The peak of the sport is the Rugby World Cup, which has been held every four years since 1989. Four nations (Australia, South Africa, England and New Zealand) have won the competition, South Africa being the last in 2007.

The first Women's World Cup was held in 1991 and won by the United States. The 2006 Women's World Cup was held in Canada and won by New Zealand. Competition will be fierce during the 2010 tournament which is taking place in England.

▲ Rugby Sevens star, Neumi Nanuku of Fiji, escapes a tackle during a match against Samoa. Rugby Sevens is a scaled-down version of rugby with only seven players a side on a full-sized rugby pitch. It's all about amazing attacking rugby and is great to watch.

Club teams compete in their own country whilst the best may play abroad as well. The Heineken Cup is the biggest competition for clubs in Europe. In the southern half of the world, the Super 14 is the top competition for the best South African, Australian and New Zealand clubs.

Every four years, a special team is assembled from Wales, Scotland, Ireland and England. Called the British and Irish Lions, it tours one of the three big rugby nations in the southern hemisphere – Australia, New Zealand and, in 2009, South Africa. Being picked as a member of that team is a great honour.

Where next?

These websites and books will help you to find out more about rugby.

http://news.bbc.co.uk/sport2/hi/rugby_union/default.stm
BBC Sport's rugby pages have news and results as well as skills videos and games.

http://www.irishrugby.ie/9683_9684.php
You can find out all about tag rugby and how to play it at this website.

http://www.smallblacks.com/
A great website for budding All Blacks (New Zealand) players, it includes video tips, games and player of the week profiles.

http://aru.rugby.com.au/onlinecoaching
The website of the Australian Rugby Union has skills and drills for young players.

http://www.rugbyworldcup.com/index.html
This is the official website of the 2011 Rugby World Cup, which is to be held in New Zealand.

http://www.rbs6nations.com/en/home.php
You can learn all about the Six Nations competition at this website. It has lots of great video highlights as well.

http://www.irb.com/rankings/full.html
See where your country is ranked against others at the International Rugby Board's official website.

Books
Rugby: A New Fan's Guide to the Game, the Teams and the Players by Paul Morgan (A & C Black, 2008)
A clear guide to how the sport is played.

Making of a Champion: Rugby Union Star by Andrew Langley (Heinemann, 2004)
This book tells you all about how top players train, prepare and play in big matches.

Rugby words

charge down block an opponent's kick with your body, hands or arms

conversion a kick taken after a try is scored which, if successful, is worth two points

drop kick a type of kick in which the ball is dropped to the ground and kicked on the half-volley just as it bounces

dummy pass an attacking technique in which a player pretends to pass the ball but actually keeps hold of it

knock-on when the ball travels forward and hits the ground after touching a player's hand or arm

maul similar to a ruck (see below), but with the tackled player remaining upright and other players joining around the player

possession when one team has the ball under control

ruck a situation that can happen after a tackle when players make contact over the ball on the ground

sidestep a sudden change of direction to the side so that the attacker with the ball can run past a defender

tap tackle a firm tap of the opponent's ankle or foot by a defender's hand

try a score worth five points. A try is scored when the attacking team touches the ball down in the opposing team's in-goal area

Index

Numbers in **bold** refer to pictures.